Fallschirmjäger in ACTION

CREATED BY **Uwe Feist**
CAPTIONS **Norman Harms**
UNIFORM ILLUSTRATION **Ron Volstadt**

Squadron/Signal Publications

ISBN 0-89747-051-6

If you have any photographs of the aircraft, armor, soldiers or ships of any nation, particularly wartime snapshots, why not share them with us and help make Squadron/Signal's books all the more interesting and complete in the future. Any photograph sent to us will be copied and the original returned. The donor will be fully credited for any photos used. Please indicate if you wish us not to return the photos. Please send them to: Squadron/Signal Publications, Inc., 1115 Crowley Dr., Carrollton, TX 75011-5010.

Photo Credit:
    Bundesarchiv
    Squadron/Signal Archive
    Norm E. Harms
    Uwe Feist Archive
    K. U. Klink
    Kurt Rieger

Introduction

The concept of landing military forces via airborne methods, as we shall see, is not a new one. On the other hand, the thought behind the concept has only within recent times been proven to be of sound military value, that is, proven under actual combat conditions. Although other nations had experimented with parachute landing of combat forces prior to the beginning of the Second World War, it remained for the German **Fallschirmjäger** (paratroopers) to establish the military precedent and total practicability of this unique method of troop deployment on the battlefield. It is due to their efforts and in particular those extended by General Student, who commanded all German parachute forces during WW II, that the concept was proven in fact, and accepted for a valuable military tool.

Opposition on various levels within the organizational structure of the German Wehrmacht had to be overcome before final acceptance would be achieved. General Student's ideas concerning the development and impending service use of his parachutists are, in general, closely akin to those put forth by General Guderian when the latter prepared the groundwork for the future German panzer forces of WW II (see Squadron/Signal Publications TIGERS IN ACTION). In each case the fullest applications, as outlined by the creators, were not carried out. One can but wonder, if these leaders had been allowed a greater degree of freedom governing their charges, what the final outcome of the Second World War could have been.

In the case of the **Fallschirmjägers,** their greatest triumph, the aerial conquest of the island of Crete, was shortly to be eclipsed by their own decline in operations as an air dropped or air landed force. Curiously, however, while their designed operational function diminished in scope, their numerical strength was increased beyond that with which they had entered the conflict of WW II. The decline in intended operations came not as a result of their actions, any lack of aggressiveness or even through the substantial losses which they suffered during the battle of Crete, although this last point did enter into considerations. Rather, their demise came as an around the corner order of the German Commander-in-Chief, Adolf Hitler. Shortly after the Crete campaign, Hitler spoke with General Student and advised him that based on **my judice,** the element of surprise had been exhausted, therefore the days of the paratroopers were over, there would be no further airborne drops. Hitler presisted in this view point until such time as the Allies had demonstrated conclusively that the day of the paratrooper had indeed not passed. Such a quirk of fate! German airborne demonstrations in Holland, Greece and especially Crete, had been the guiding light for the Allies to build and develop their own airborne forces.

Immediately, Hitler demanded the expansion of the **Fallschirm** arm and though the expansion of the force could be undertaken, the day of the German paratrooper, with the exception of small, minor air landings, had been expended. The overall war situation had drastically changed by 1943 and the balance of power no longer lay with German arms. By the end of the war a total of eleven **Fallschirmjäger** divisions had been formed. Expansion to this number had been accomplished by using a cadre of existing units to form the core of the new divisions. As such, the number of fully trained, jump qualified, paratroopers never caught up to the actual number of personnel formed into these units. Never-the-less, these units, now committed to traditional ground fighting, continued to give a good accounting of themselves during combat and earned a high degree of respect from their Allied opponents.

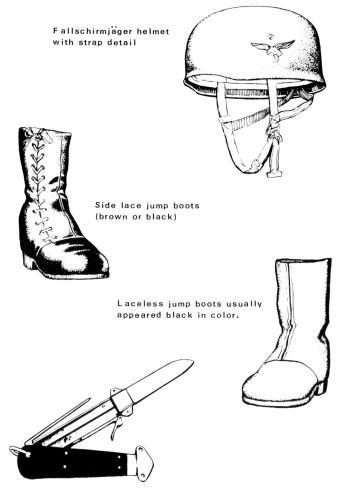

Fallschirmjäger helmet with strap detail

Side lace jump boots (brown or black)

Laceless jump boots usually appeared black in color.

Fallschirmjäger gravity knife, carried in pocket by right knee of trousers.

Through the eye of the camera lens we shall examine and trace the history of the FALLSCHIRMJÄGER IN ACTION. Here, a group of parachutists and an Army companion, converse with a German war correspondent/combat photographer, a member of the **Propaganda Kompanie.**

Complete training of German paratroopers, due to the nature of the mission(s) assigned to them, included that for ground operations as an infantryman and for landing from the air. Hours of practicing the proper exiting of the transport aircraft by means of static fuselages, or as here a doorway mock-up, instilled confidence in the trainee.

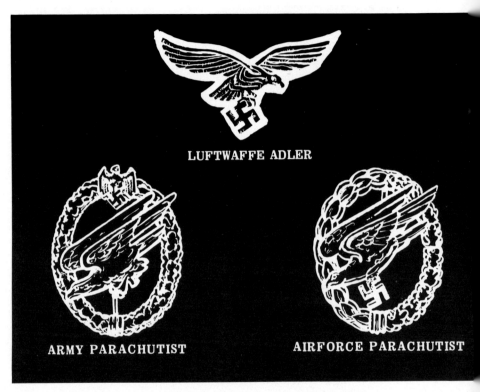

LUFTWAFFE ADLER

ARMY PARACHUTIST

AIRFORCE PARACHUTIST

After completion of the initial phases of basic training which included techniques of landing, handling the parachute harness, parachute packing and exiting methods, these trainees prepare for their first jump from an aircraft. Rubber knee pads and the padded Fallschirmjäger helmet are in place as they buckle on the parachute harness. Elbow pads and gauntlets will be added later. Both the early jump smock, the step in model, and the later snap fastening model in camouflage pattern, are viewed.

Waiting for their turn, this group of students observes the descent of a prior group. The purpose of the close fitting jump smock about the thighs, afforded either by the tailored model or the snap fastenings, is to prevent the smock from "ballooning" during the air drop. Trousers are bloused into the top of the front laced jump boot. An earlier model of the jump boot laced up the side.

FALLSCHIRMSCHULE
STENDAL

Normal jump height for German paratroopers, about 400 feet - approximately that which is being flown by the Ju 52 in the center of the photo, allowed for a quick descent and as such reduced the amount of time during which they were exposed to enemy ground fire. Dropping at such a low altitude required a chute which would open automatically via a static-line. The first such parachute, Model RZ 1, had been followed in service by the improved RZ 16 and later the RZ 36, the latter model viewed here.

General Student's airborne command included not only the facilities for training his personnel in the proper jump methods but also included the support units necessary to this end such as the transport air groups. At the beginning of the war, six air transport groups, each equipped with 52 Ju 52's were an organic part of **7. Fliegerdivision.** The troop carrying capability of the venerable "Tante Ju" was 12 to 16 fully equipped men. Eleven of these paratroopers, led by their jumpmaster, walk to their aircraft prior to a practice jump.

Boarding the Ju 52 required both hands. The static line of the parachute is carried in the mouth so as to not foul when entering. The wing/bar insignia of rank indicates that the second man in line is an **Oberleutnant** (1st Lieutenant). During the first years of the paratroopers, all personnel from Private to General were required to qualify by completing the necessary six jumps. During the late war years, conditions circumvented this qualification.

On the jumpmaster's command, **"Fertig zum Sprung"** (Ready to Jump), the jumpers stand to the door, having already attached their static lines. Counting the number of static lines exposed at the door, we find that this **Unteroffizier** (Sergeant), single wing insignia of rank, will be the fifth man to leave the aircraft.

Technological improvements in aircraft design led many Luftwaffe first line aircraft types to be relegated to second line duties, such as training. While best remembered for its role as a transport, the Junker's Ju 52 had been one of the first Luftwaffe bombers. The Do 23, shown, had also been among the first bomber designs employed by the new German Air Force. Owing to difficulties, however, it had been replaced early in its career. Jumping from this converted bomber, three stages of parachute deployment may be seen - initial jump pose (man directly under fuselage), chute beginning to open and chute opened.

Having a new weapon, such as the paratroopers, presents many problems until such time as it can be tried under combat conditions. Staged operations, i.e. combat exercises, help recognize potential problem areas but lack the element of enemy thinking and reaction. Such a case in point concerns German parachutists jumping with their weapons. The first combat drops which took place in Denmark/Norway and Holland, had the men jump without their weapons, except for a pistol. Rifles and ammunition, machine guns, etc. were packed in separate containers dropped with the men. Becoming separated from these containers could and did spell disaster. On Crete the same technique had been employed and many men were lost attempting to recover the equipment canisters. The lesson had been learned the hard way, thereafter the troops jumped with their rifles and submachine guns, heavier equipment and additional ammunition still packed in the canisters.

"Fallschirmbombe", the paratroopers equipment canister, being recovered after a drop. These canisters were not restricted to use only during airborne operations. Later during the war, it became necessary to supply isolated units from the air using the "Fallschirmbombe."

10

With the completion of their sixth practice jump, the trainee became a fully qualified paratrooper and received his jump certificate and awarded the **Fallschirmschützen-Abzeichen,** Parachutist's Badge. An Army and Luftwaffe badge existed for their respective personnel qualified for jumping. To maintain his status, six additional jumps per year were required. From this photograph, we can see that the German parachute is worn much lower than Allied counterparts, static line worn over the left shoulder. No reserve parachute is included, another difference from British and U.S. paratroops.

The chute harness of the Fallschirmjägers differed from that of other Luftwaffe personnel in that the shrouds of the parachute joined together at a point above the wearer and not at the shoulders. This placement created a high center of gravity and resulted in the head first dive from the airplane being necessary to assist in absorbing the opening shock of the parachute.

Standing at "Rest" these Fallschirmjäger graduates form one of the elite arms of the German Wehrmacht. By virtue of the qualifications needed to enter parachute school and of the training they received, each and everyone of these men could be a noncommissioned or officer rank in a regular ground formation.

(Above left) While the Russians were the first to develop a military assault glider, the Germans were the first to use such an aircraft under actual combat conditions. Development of the DFS 230 had been undertaken as a means of delivering an assault from the air whereby the troops would not be separated from their weapons and also would be able to carry their heavier armament directly into combat.

(Left) Norway below. A member of **Leutnant** von Brandis' company stands to the door awaiting the order to jump on Sola Air Base outside Stavanger. At this early date in the war both the Luftwaffe insignia, diving eagle, and the German National insignia, black, white, red, shield are worn on the steel helmet. After 1941 the National insignia phased from use, leaving only the Wehrmacht insignia on the helmet, left side.

As mentioned previously, the head first, spread eagle, position had been found necessary to lessen the opening shock of the parachute. A form some what similar to this is used today by Sky Divers, sport parachute enthusiasts.

Difficulties in receiving seaborne reinforcements at Narvik, led to **Hauptmann** (Captain) Walther's battalion being dropped to assist General Dietl's 3rd Mountain Division. This **Jäger** receives assistance in gathering his chute from a member of the German forces already at Narvik. Additional drops had been planned for the Norwegian Campaign but were called off after the complete evacuation of Allied forces following the collapse of France in June 1940.

"WESERÜBUNG" NARVIK
APRIL, 1940

Allied assistance to the Norwegians consisted of two British divisions along with French and Polish units. Joining with the Norwegians, these forces gradually forced General Dietl to withdraw his own forces until promised reinforcements could be brought into play. The town of Bjørnfjell became an important supply base for 3rd Mountain Division, laying along the railroad from Sweden to Narvik. **Fallschrimjägers** arrive at Bjørnfjell and prepare to move against Norwegian units approaching from the north.

Oberleutnant Fritz Becker gathers the men of his command after their jump in the Narvik area. Spare ammunition for their machine gun is carried in the metal cans, rifle ammunition is carried in the bandoliers suspended around the neck. The winter had not yet departed these far northern reaches of Norway in May and further increased the difficulties encountered by German forces.

EBEN-EMAEL
MAY 10, 1940

Formed in November 1939, **"Sturmabteilung Koch"** had been created for the specific task of neutralizing the Belgium fortifications on the Albert Canal, Eben Emael. Their assault would not come via a parachute drop but rather through first use of the DFS 230 assault glider. Sequestered on their home base of Hildesheim, intensive training prepared them in the use of the DFS 230. The advantage of using a glider can be derived from a close examination of this photo. The four **Unteroffiziers** (Sergeants) emerge from their safely landed 230 fully equipped with MP 40 submachine guns and MG 34 ready for action. They do not have to wait to find a weapons canister.

Ammunition became a precious item in the Narvik area. Although German forces held the railroad from Bjørnfjell to Narvik, supplies could only be moved to Hundalen by means of the railroad, thereafter they had to be carried along the railroad right of way the remaining 15 miles to Narvik. This remaining section of the railroad lay exposed to shelling by warships of the Royal Navy. The sign on the building in the background identifies it as the Tourist Station at Bjørnfjell. The airborne troops taking count of their ammunition supplies did not consider this a tourist trip.

Disembarking their 230, the pilot leaps from the cockpit, MP 40 in hand, followed by the glider's gunner with the first of the glider troops emerging from the aircraft's open door. Defensive armament of the DFS 230 consisted of a single 7.92mm MG 15 mounted on the upper deck of the forward fuselage, viewed directly behind the open cockpit canopy. The flexible mount of the MG 15 allow it to supply supporting fire for the occupants of the 230 and could be removed to join in an assault. Later two MG 34's could be affixed to the nose of the glider for increased firepower.

Full size mock-ups of the Eben Emael defense systems were devised for the complete training program. Climbing over the concrete and wire emplacement, an **Unteroffizier** is provided covering fire by the **Feldwebel's** (Technical Sergeant) MP 40. Every man in the **"Sturmabteilung"** had been thoroughly trained in every phase of the Eben Emael operation in order that he knew not only his own duty but others as well.

BELGIUM AND HOLLAND

Use of Germany's airborne forces in Norway had been a matter of urgency, for Operation **Weserubung** preceeded only a few days an intended British landing at Narvik. Prior to their service in Norway/Denmark, Student had been instructed to prepare his Division for use in the upcoming Western Offensive, code name "Case Yellow," the attack against France. Student felt that their premier in Scandinavia would betray some of their surprise element and alert the Allies to possible future airborne actions. Any objections which he could raise had to tempered, for the **OKW, Oberkommando der Wehrmacht** - Armed Forces High Command, still held some doubts concerning the exploitation of this new weapon.

During the winter months of 1939-40 and into the Spring of 1940, British and French forces lay installed in and about the Maginot Line. A frontal assault on these impressive defensive works, the finest conceived by man at that time, could only spell disaster for the attacker. Lulled into a sense of security by this fact, the Allies were about to be awakened from their long winter sleep. German plans did not consider a strong frontal attack as the path to France. Rather, as had happened in 1914, a flanking move would open the magic gate. The attack plan, as adopted, called for a broader version of the von Schlieffen Plan used in 1941, Belgium and Luxembourg would again be avenues of approach. To forestall any possibility of restricted flow of men and material through these two countries, as had occured in 1914, Holland had become a target as well.

Operating as a part of Army Group B (Generaloberst von Bock), 6th Army (Generaloberst von Reichenau) had been assigned the task of forcing a crossing of the Maas river, penetrate Belgian defenses towards Tirlemont and isolate the fortified area around Luettich (Liége). One of the keypoint Belgian defenses, Fortress Eben Emael on the Albert Canal, and bridges over the canal itself, would have to be taken to insure the rapid completion of 6th Army's mission.

Neutralization of Eben Emael and securing the bridge crossings had been entrusted to a special parachute unit, about battalion strength, organized for this purpose, "Sturmabteilung Koch", "Assault Group Koch". From its formation in November 1939, strict security measures were employed to protect and keep secret the existance of this group. The group had been all but totally cut off from the outside world, no leave being granted and strict mail censorship imposed. Training occupied their full time, every man knew not only his own job but the others as well.

Eben Emael had been well designed to resist ground assault and offer protection to the bridges. 75mm and 120mm guns in armored rotating cupolas, 60mm anti-tank guns and heavy machine gun emplacements and the ability of the 1200 man garrison to move from section to section by way of underground tunnels would seem to have taken every contingency into account. Eben Emael can be likened to Hitler's "Festung Europe," with very strong walls but no roof, that fatal flaw that doomed the 3rd Reich itself would be proved in 1940. While the bridges would be less defensible, provisions had been made such that the defenders could easily destroy them by means of prepared and emplaced demolition charges.

During the early morning hours of May 10, 1940, forty-two Ju 52's stood ready and waiting on the airfields of Ostheim and Butzweilerhof near Cologne. "Assault Group Koch" arrived and embarked not in the transport aircraft but in the DFS 230 gliders behind each of the Ju 52's. The paratroops would not jump onto their respective targets, rather first use would be made of the newly developed DFS 230 assault glider, the troops landing on their objective. A conventional parachute jump has the tendency of spreading the attacking force over a wide area, concentration of the attackers had to be assured.

Captain Koch had broken his Assault Group into four distinct elements, each with its own specific duty to perform. These were as follows:

"Assault Group Concrete"(Leutnant Schacht) - secure the concrete bridge over the Albert Canal at Vroenhoven and hold until arrival of Army forces.

"Assault Group Iron" (Leutnant Schachter) - secure the bridge at Kanne.

"Assault Group Steel" (Oberleutnant Altman) - secure the steel bridge at Veldwezelt.

"Assault Group Granite" (Oberleutnant Witzig) - eliminate the outer fortifications of Eben Emael and hold until arrival of Army Engineer Battalion 51. All members of the Granite Group were trained and experienced combat engineers.

By 0530 hours, the first gliders of Group Steel touched down near the bridge at Veldwezelt. After a furious battle the paratroops stormed the bridge and removed the demolition charges. Efforts by the Belgians to retake the bridge were beaten back by the **Fallschirmjägers** with support from elements of the Luftwaffe's VII Air Corps. Due to Dutch forces being able to destroy the bridges over the Maas river, Army relief forces would not reach Group Steel until the afternoon of the next day.

Outnumbered by the Belgians, Group Concrete's attack carried their objective and prevented its demolition by a matter of a few seconds. Counterattacks and an attempt to destroy the structure with artillery fire failed, the bridge remained in German hands. The promised Army forces arrived at 2140 hours the same day.

The performances of Groups Steel and Concrete, unfortunately, would not be repeated by Group Iron. Just as their gliders were setting down, the defenders in Eben Emael touched off the explosive charges and destroyed the Kanne bridge.

Witzig's Group Granite met strong resistance from the fortress defenders.

Within ten minutes of their landing, ten positions had been suppressed and with a majority of the fort's artillery now out of action, the full question had not yet been decided. The Belgian commander, Major Jottrand, called down fire on his own position to dislodge the Germans. The attackers were now forced to seek protection and assume a defensive posture. The battle raged throughout the day and night. At 0700 hours the next morning, an assault party from the Army's engineer battalion had fought its way to join the weary Para-engineers. At noon an attack was mounted against the remaining fortified positions. An hour and fifteen minutes later, Major Jottrand and his 1200 men command surrendered.

The Victors of Eben Emael. Hitler personally presented the Knights Cross to the outstanding personalities of the Eben Emael Operation. Standing to Hitler's right is Major Koch (promoted for his part in the operation) and to Koch's right is Captain Witzig. To Hitler's left is **Oberleutnant** Meissner. The variation in the first issue Luftwaffe jump smock may be viewed here as well, Major Koch wears the pattern featuring only a single zippered pocket on the breast, Lt. Meissner's smock has two.

The German 18th Army had been charged with the capture of Holland, thereby protecting the northern flank of the main German thrust into France. Numerically inferior to the Dutch defenders, the completion of this commission lay in the ability of Student's forces being able to secure and hold for some length of time key bridges across the Maas and Rhine rivers. The Dutch must not be allowed the opportunity to destroy these crossings.

Excluding the airborne battalion put to use against Eben Emael and the bridges over the Albert Canal, the bulk of General Student's 7th Division, four battalions of some 4000 men, had been reinforced for the Dutch operations with 12,000 men of the Army's 22nd Infantry Division, also trained in air landings. The responsibility of assailing the bridges at Moerdijk, Dordrecht and Rotterdam had been given the paratroops. They were to also supplement the landings at three airfields, Valkenburg, Ypenburg and Ockenburg, near the Hague, from which air landed personnel were to attempt to seize the Ministry of War, Royal Palace and other government buildings. Student decided to command in person the bridge operations leaving the forces engaged in the Hague under command of the 22nd Divisional commander, General-leutnant Graf Sponeck.

452 Ju 52's were to be used in transporting the mass of men and material to their objectives. In the case of troops landing at airfields, it would be necessary for the transports to make several trips before the full allotment of personnel could be brought in. Alerted to German airborne tactics, evidenced in Denmark and Norway, the Dutch had prepared their airfields to offer resistance against a direct air landed attack.

Hundreds upon hundreds of parachute canopies blossomed over the Dutch countryside on the morning of May 10, 1940. The peace and quiet of the scene had been broken some time before by the screech of Ju 87 dive bombers and Bf 109 fighters, softening up objectives. Stillness would not return for four days. Flying at 400 feet, the paratroopers had a brief drop to their respective goals. After a short but sharp fight the highway and railway bridges over the Diep at Moerkijk fell into German hands. At Dordrecht, the initial gain of the bridges were lost to a Dutch counterattack; thereafter elements of the 1st Parachute Regiment, in association with 3rd Battalion, 16th Infantry Regiment (landed at Waalhaven) would contest ownership of the town with Dutch forces for three days. Waalhaven airfield lay to the south-west of the city of Rotterdam. Seizure of this field by the 3rd Battalion, 1st Parachute Regiment prepared the way for the arrival of 16th Infantry Regiment and the subsequent taking of the Willems bridge over the river Maas. Heavy and bitter defensive fighting took place but the air and bridgeheads held.

Chances for a rapid consolidation of German forces in the Hague area were thwarted by Dutch defenses and prepared airfield obstacles. The inability to land on some of the designated fields forced many transports to put down along side roads and in open fields. This action, spreading the attacking forces, resulted in the creation of even greater confusion among the Dutch defenders but also resulted in numerous machines being written off, and dissipated the German attack. Casualties sustained during the original landings plus those incurred from stout resistance seriously weakened the German forces' offensive ability. Irregardless, these forces and their paratrooper comrade-in-arms, held against all odds until contact had been established with advance parties of the 18th Army.

On May 14, 1940 the Netherlands surrendered. The price of the airborne victory had been small in comparison to the total number of personnel involved, only 180 killed. There had been one important casualty though, General Student himself. Three hours after the cease-fire in Rotterdam, Student had been critically wounded by a stray bullet as he attempted to stop a detachment from **Leibstandarte Adolf Hitler** firing upon a group of surrendering Dutch who were bringing their arms to a collection point.

HOLLAND
MAY 10, 1940

Men of the 7th Air Division move with their equipment to the staging area for the drop on Holland. Student's full force would be involved in the Dutch operations, they had an important mission to perform. Discounting Koch's detachment, which number slightly less than a battalion, four battalions of some 4000 men would drop on Holland. To supplement the air landings 12,000 men of the Army's 22nd Infantry Division would also be used in the airborne phase of the capture of Holland.

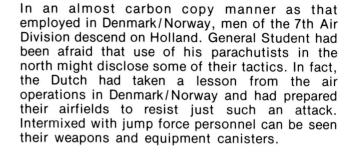

In an almost carbon copy manner as that employed in Denmark/Norway, men of the 7th Air Division descend on Holland. General Student had been afraid that use of his parachutists in the north might disclose some of their tactics. In fact, the Dutch had taken a lesson from the air operations in Denmark/Norway and had prepared their airfields to resist just such an attack. Intermixed with jump force personnel can be seen their weapons and equipment canisters.

This MG 34 mounted on a tripod, serves in the role of a heavy machine gun. The various components of the weapon have been gathered from the weapon canisters and assembled. The machine crew rapidly gathers additional supplies of ammunition and will provide defensive fire for the air dropping zone.

Seizure of the airfield at Waalhaven had been accomplished by members of the 3rd Battalion, 1st Parachute Regiment dropped right onto the field itself. Thereafter, elements of the 16th Infantry Regiment landed and proceeded to their objective, the Willems bridge over the river Maas. The fight for this bridge became such that no living thing would cross it for almost five days. In the meantime, members of both these units were also engaged in fighting for the town of Dordrecht, the bridges there having been retaken by Dutch forces. As indicated by the road sign on the right, these members of the 1st Parachute Regiment and 16th Infantry Regiment are very near to both battles.

(right)   Awards befell the victors of Holland, again presented by Hitler. By the conclusion of WW II, the **Fallschirmtruppe** would be presented with 201 Knights Crosses, 27 Oak Leaves to Knights Cross, 7 Swords and one Diamonds Award. General Ramcke received the Diamonds Award on September 19, 1944 for his defense of the city of Brest.

(Above right) Fallschirmjäger of the III. Battalion Fallschirmjäger Regiment I (III Bat. FJR I) escorting a group of Dutch infantry men into captivity. Rotterdam, May 11, 1940.

Heavier weapons, such as this 3.7cm anti-tank gun, could not be parachuted. Their appearance in battle depended upon the ability of the German forces being able to secure a suitable landing field where additional troops, supplies and weapons of a heavier nature could be brought in via transport aircraft. Stubborn Dutch resistance had denied free access to the airfields in the Hague area, leaving only Waalhaven for total German use. At one time during the battle for Rotterdam, upon order of Student who was personally directing his forces, the defending German forces at Waalhaven were ordered to another sector leaving the base undefended. This gamble paid off, the Dutch did not counterattack.

A notable member of the **Fallschirmtruppe** was Max Schmeling, former heavyweight boxing champion of the world. Schmeling, shown here during a winter training exercise, jumped on Crete as part of the 3rd Parachute Regiment. Clearly shown in the photo is the side lace jump boots.

The fact that a former world champion boxer served in the German Wehrmacht did not escape the attention of Dr. Goebbels' propaganda machine. Schmeling appeared in many of the German wartime publications, even being featured on the cover of "Signal" magazine on one occasion. The **Unteroffizier** accompanying this group of **Fallschirmjagers** is himself a paratrooper, indicated by the Parachutists Badge, worn on his left pocket and the Flying Personnel specialty badge worn on the left sleeve.

Airborne troops await the word to board their transports. Each of the men's parachutes have been carefully packed by its owner, once more teaching the individual to rely on his own abilities. The Ju 52 in the background belongs to I./KGzbV 1.

KRETA

MAY 20, 1941

In September 1940 General Student had recovered from his wounds and been returned to duty. The overall attitude of the High Command had changed considerably during his absence. The ad hoc airborne corps which he had commanded in Holland/Belgium had been formalized becoming **Fliegerkorps XI.** Expansion and training continued such that Fliegerdivision 7 comprised three full regiments with a full assortment of support and administrative units attached. Also formed under corp troops was a training or demonstration regiment who would be capable of going into combat either by parachute or glider means. Filling out 11th Air Corps complement of forces, 22nd Infantry Division remained on detached service from the Army under Student's control.

The cancellation of plans for the invasion of England, Operation Sea Lion, soon focussed attention towards the east and Russia. Hitler's overall plans for Operation Barbarossa were disrupted by the movement of Italian forces into Greece in October 1940. Mussolini had decided to gain a share of the glory on his own. In so doing, German involvement became necessary when the Italian attack faltered and verged on collapse. A portion of the rescue forces sent to Greece included 2nd Fallschirmjager Regiment under command of Colonel Sturm.

On April 25, 1941, 1st and 2nd Battalions, 2 Parachute Regiments along with an engineer platoon and a medical company, took off from Larissa with the objective of attacking the bridge over the Corinth canal and thereby cutting off the British line of withdrawal to the Peloponnesus. After a brief fight, the bridge lay in German control only to be destroyed when a lucky strike by a British anti-aircraft round detonated the explosives placed on the bridge. Quick work on the part of the Para-engineers soon had a temporary crossing in place by the time of the arrival of the first panzer forces. Had this strike been made but two days earlier, it is possible that the entire British force could have been cut off.

The island of Crete is the fifth largest in the Mediterranean. From a military view, the island dominates the eastern portion of the Mediterranean being 60 miles from Greece and 350 miles from Egypt. The British had secured the island after the Italian invasion of Greece. It had been their intention to garrison the island and use it as a major supply base. In British hands, the island continually represented a serious threat to the Rumanian oil fields, within range of RAF bombers, vital to the German war effort and exposed the southern flank of the forces about to invade Russia. Some of the British and Greek forces withdrawn from the Greek mainland were used to strengthen those troops already present on the island.

On April 20, Student submitted a plan of attack for the airborne occupation of Crete to Goring. At about the same time, the Army High Command had prepared an assault plan for use against Malta, an equally important position. Hitler had the final decision in the matter and in Fuhrer Order No. 28, dated April 25, 1941, the objective was stated as follows:

"The occupation of the Island of Crete, as a base for the conduct of war against England by air in the Eastern Mediterranean, is to be prepared."

Operation **Merkur** (Mercury) had been born.

As a part of the above directive, the Commander-in-Chief of the Luftwaffe assumed control of the operation; under his command the commander-in-chief Fourth Air Fleet (Generaloberst Loehr) was to conduct the operation. Only the forces of 11th Air Corps were to be used and the operation must take place during May - no further delays could be tolerated in Operation Barbarossa.

Some 600 transport aircraft had been made available for the Crete Operation **Merkur**. Loss reports indicate that one-third of this number were damaged with more than half this number permanently lost or written off as no longer fit for service. In terms of numbers, both the paratroopers and army suffered high losses, over 3,250 German soldiers killed or missing and 3,400 wounded. The British lost 10,700 prisoners, the Greeks 5,000, while appr. 5,000 British and Greek servicemen died in action, not including the casualties at sea.

All elements of 11th Air Corps were to be involved. It would be an undertaking of some measure just to assemble the entirety of the Corps, they had become spread over large areas from Germany to Greece. At this time the Table of Organization for 7th Air Division included three parachute regiments, each of three battalions; one assault regiment equipped with transport gliders and consisting of four battalions; one parachute anti-tank battalion; one parachute artillery battalion; one parachute anti-aircraft machine gun battalion; one signals battalion; and one parachute medical battalion. 22nd Infantry Division, stationed in Bucharest, could not be moved south due to the clogged transportation system, the panzer forces were being assembled for the Russian offensive and by Hitler's expressed orders they were not to be interfered with. 5th Mountain Division (General-leutnant Ringel), reinforced with a third regiment from 6th Mountain Division, both these units already in Greece, replaced 22nd Infantry Division in the forthcoming Operation Merkur. Altogether some 22,000 men were involved.

11th Air Corps supplied its own transport sections, 622 Ju 52's and 600 gliders. The preparation of these aircraft for the coming battle proved to be a minor technological miracle. The greater majority of the planes had been in service hauling cargo to various places in the Balkans and Greece and were in need of major thru minor overhauls. Working around the clock, maintenance personnel completed this task and the transports stood ready when needed.

Fliegerkorps VIII (General von Richthofen) added two bomber wings - 180 bombers; one dive bomber wing - 120 Ju 87's; one fighter wing - 110 Bf 109's; one long range fighter wing - 60 Bf 110's; and two reconnaissance squadrons.

Seaborne elements had been organized to transport equipment and personnel which could not be brought in by air means. Sixty-three motor sailers and 7 steamships formed this sea transport echelon and their safety became the charge of the Italian Navy, who deployed 4 submarines, 4 MAS patrol torpedo boats, 8 minesweepers and 12 torpedo boats. During the course of events, these sea forces were either destroyed by the Royal Navy outright or forced to return to their bases and played no part in the ensuing battle, full credit and direction of the battle's outcome belongs to the airborne units.

The attacking force had been divided into three major groups. These groups and their objectives were:

> **Western Group** (General-Major Meindl) - the airfield at Maleme.
>
> **Center Group** (General-Leutnant Sussman, commander of 7th Air Division) - Canea and Retimo airfields.
>
> **Eastern Group** (Oberst Brauer, until relieved by General Ringel) - Heraklion airfield.

Sufficient aircraft transport and gliders did not exist to enable the entire force to land at a single time. As such three waves of attacks had been planned, Maleme and Canea the first wave, Retimo and Heraklion attacked by the second wave and the third wave supplying forces to all four airfields.

Defenders on Crete numbered 27,500 British and 14,000 Greek troops under command of General Freyberg, a New Zealander. Use of the paratroopers at Corinth had disclosed their presence in the Mediterranean area. It stood to reason that any attack mounted against Crete would involve paratroopers. Freyberg, therefore, positioned his forces to cover this possibility at the four airbases and also to repel any naval landings at Suda Bay. The stage had now been set for another page of military history to unfold.

Paving the way for the airborne troops, General von Richthofen's fighters and bombers subjected Maleme, Canea and Suda Bay to heavy low-level attacks. At 0715 hours, May 20, 1941, the first gliders touched down outside the airfield at Maleme. The parachutists and gliders continued to come down all over the island's target areas. Concentrating their forces had become difficult, the defensive fire was heavy and German losses mounted steadily. The situation grew worse. Communications with 11th Corps Headquarters broke down,

Headquarters could not know the desperate condition in which the first wave had found themselves. The second wave went in as planned and suffered even heavier losses.

By evening none of the prime objectives had been taken, though a portion of the airfield at Maleme did belong to the German forces. The portion in and under their control was not adequate enough to permit the badly needed reinforcements and supplies to land.

During the night the paratroopers grimly held to their positions. With the coming of morning, the Luftwaffe fighters and bombers again took to the air and helped pin down British forces. Several Ju 52's had crashlanded near Maleme and from these victims of the battle, the attackers were able to recover ammunition supplies, initial stocks of which had all but been exhausted during the battle the day before. At noon, Oberst (Colonel) Ramcke and a reserve battalion dropped west of Maleme, suffering heavy casualties. With this added assistance the

The Junkers Ju 52 ("Tante Ju") could carry twelve fully equipped Fallschirmjägers into action.

Hill 107 dominated the scene near Maleme. Major Koch's gliderborne troops landed along side the hill but were not able to fully regroup for an assault on the New Zealand position. Many of the weapons canisters had been lost or due to enemy fire could not be recovered. Climaxing the battle for Hill 107, two groups of the Assault Regiment stormed the hill positions and reached the top that evening using pistols and hand grenades. Having completely exhausted their supply of ammunition the paratroopers would have been hard pressed to repel even the smallest counterattack. With no such action on the part of the British taking place during the night, the position of the Germans improved when an ammunition carrying Ju 52 landed on the Maleme airfield. Thereafter they were able to fully secure the field and allow a continued flow of supplies and troops to arrive.

1940-1942

PLATE II

PLATE I

PLATE III

Ron Volstad

1942-1943

PLATE V

PLATE IV

PLATE VI

Ron Volstad

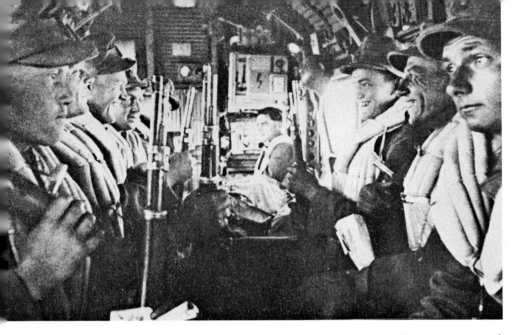

Wearing life jackets identical to those issued to crews of transports, bombers and flying boats, these members of the 5th Mountain Division fly from their Greek bases to the recently capture field at Maleme. The battle for Crete would not end for some time but with that single airfield in German hands the tide had turned.

remaining portion of the airfield was assaulted and fell. Air landed troops of 5th Mountain Division began to arrive in the afternoon. The battle continued but with an airfield in their hands and fresh troops and material available, the Germans had gained the upper hand.

Withdrawing across the mountains and southwards towards Sphakia, British and Greek troops kept up their fight. At Sphakia on May 28, units of the Royal Navy began evacuating what men they could. It would be impossible to remove all units. By the time the evacuation operation terminated on June 1 some 16,500 troops had been snatched from the island and returned to Egypt.

The overall campaign had been costly to both sides. German losses were 3,250 killed or missing with 3,400 wounded. British losses were 15,743 killed, wounded or captured. 14,000 Italian prisoners of war were liberated. The Royal Navy, operating in close support had lost over 2,000 men, 3 cruisers and 6 destroyers.

To commemorate this battle a special arm band had been designed and was issued to all German forces who had participated during hostilities. One can be assured that it was worn with a great deal of pride.

■ ■ ■

Projected to be replaced in service by the MG 42, the MG 34 saw continuing use throughout the entire Second World War. Both the MG 34 and 42 were versatile weapons being able to fill the light, with bipod mount, medium and heavy, with tripod mount, roles. Additional accessories allowed these weapons to be converted to function as an anti-aircraft weapon. Here a MG 34, heavy MG mount with telescopic sight, is served by an airborne crew in the hills of Italy.

Major Karl-Lothar Schulz Kommandeur of III. Bataillon, Flieger-Div. 7 and Oberleutnant Horst Kerfin at Heraklion, Crete Mai 28, 1941.

Obergefreiter (Corporal) stands guard over some of the Commonwealth soldiers captured on Crete. No tropical uniforms were then available to German units in the Mediterranean area. Some measure of comfort has been obtained by removing his jump smock and reveals for us the special pocket for his gravity knife in the right pant leg.

Captured British vehicles are ultimately utilized by the Fallschirmjäger, here a Morris truck is pulling a 37mm PAK.

In the thickest fighting for the island of Crete, the battle did not allow much breathing space for the **Fallschirmjägers.** Meals became a matter of eating when you could.

A Fallschirmjäger major is receiving the Iron Cross First-Class from General Student, Kommandeur of the XI. Flieger (Luftlande) Korps, responsible for the conquest of Crete.

Using an Italian 47/32 anti-tank gun, model 37, two **Jägers** prepare a coastal position. This particular weapon had a range of 3,800 yards firing HE ammunition and an effective range of 220 to 1,100 yards using AP or HE. It could be used in an infantry support role as well as anti-tank; it was inferior to the British 2-pounder in hitting power.

Allied air superiority in the Mediterranean forced some strange adoptions of equipment to meet air attacks. Here a **Fallschirmjäger** in tropical uniform, mans an anti-aircraft position, a make-shift mount with belt fed MG 42. Note that the bipod machine gun mount has been re-positioned towards the middle of the weapon and that an anti-aircraft sight ring has also been added.

Field Marshal Kesselring, left in white Luftwaffe cap, Commander-in-Chief, South, commanded all German forces in the Mediterranean area. Fifteen German divisions were available to him for the defense of Italy when the Allies landed at Salerno, including troops of the 1st Parachute Division and "**Hermann Göring**" Division.

Flanked by two 5cm Pak 38 L/60 anti-tank guns and a Paratrooper guard of honor, Kesselring prepares for an awards ceremony, Italy, summer 1943.

Kesselring presents the Iron Cross 2nd Class to members of the Ramcke Brigade.

A 8cm schwerer Granatwerfer in action.

Towing a 37mm anti-tank gun (PAK), the 3t half-tracked prime mover, with members of the **"Hermann Göring"** Division aboard, heads for the Salerno beachhead.

Conducting a fighting withdrawal from the invasion beachhead, German units, including paratroopers, moved towards the north and the Gustav defense line. The hills and roads of Italy form natural defense lines and each and every opportunity which could be used to slow the U.S. advance was put to practice. Here a 5cm PAK 38, manned by a paratrooper crew, fires on advancing Allied tanks.

MONTE CASSINO
1944

Members of **Fallschirm-MG-Bataillon 1, 1. Fallschirmjäger-Division,** at Cassino. Organization of the Parachute MG Battalion consisted of the Battalion Staff and Signals Section plus three Machine Gun Companies. Each company included two heavy machine gun platoons, a 81mm mortar platoon and a light machine gun platoon. Personnel numbered five officers and approximately 200 enlistedmen; equipment - 2 LMG's 8 Heavy MG's and 4 Mortars.

The ammunition for both the MG 34 and 42 and the standard German rifle of WW II, the Mauser Kar 98K carbine, were identical. Common ammunition greatly eased some of the supply difficulties. Another weapon in service and common to the airborne forces and mountain troops was the Gewehr 33/40, also of 7.92mm caliber, a shorter version of the 98K. This machine gun crewman carries a 50 round belt of ammo for the machine gun and the paratrooper rifle ammo bandolier around his neck. A detailed look at the camouflage band on his helmet cover is also afforded.

During the Battle of Cassino, the advantage of height lay with the German forces. With height came observation. The Allies believed that German forces had been using the Abbey on Monte Cassino for spotting purposes, which does not seem to be the case. The Allied decision to bomb the Abbey offered the defenders the chance to move into the ruins which in turn were converted to excellent defensive positions.

A Fallschirmjäger of the II./FJR 3 in the ruins of Cassino, observing the railroad station of Cassino under artillery bombardment. Armed with a MG 42, MP 40, Luger Pistole and Stielhandgranate (potatomasher), this Jäger is ready to meet yet another assault by the allied infantry, Monte Cassino, March 16, 1944.

Fallschirmjäger in Action

The battle for Monte Cassino became the scene of a bitterly contested fight lasting four months. Many of the veteran Allied divisions were withdrawn from the Italian Campaign to lend their assistance in Operation Overlord, the invasion of France. Their absence would be felt. Apart from the decrease in the numbers of available fightingmen on the Allied side, the question of the bombing of the Abbey of St. Benedict, situated on Monte Cassino, had been a long to overcome problem for the Allied command. By order of Kesselring, no German troops were located in the Abbey proper but it appeared this position had been used for observation purposes.

A decision had been reached, on February 15, Allied bombers appeared over Cassino and unloaded their deadly cargo, the Abbey was reduced to a pile of rubble. Still the Allies were not able to take the position by direct assault. After the initial bombardment, German troops moved into the ruins of the Abbey, which then formed perfect defensive positions. The struggle continued. Using artillery bombardment, air support and tanks, attack after attack failed to attain that singular goal, Cassino. It would not be until the 11th of May that Cassino would be outflanked, finally falling on May 17. German forces, including the defending **Fallschirmjägers,** had not been defeated but had conducted another withdrawal further to the north. The Battle of Italy continued.

Cassino represented a tremendous roadblock to the Allied advance on Rome. After the breakdown in attacks on Cassino it had been decided to approach the problem from a different direction, an amphibious landing further to the north thereby outflanking the entire Gustav Line.

Cassino was called the Italian Verdun by the Germans. Between 12:30 and 20:00 hrs. (March 15, 1944), the Allied artillery fired 196,000 rounds of ammunition, enough rounds to fill 275 railroad boxcars. The expression on the faces of the two I./FJR 3 men show the traces of many days of fighting, lack of sleep and thirst.

The most famous German submachine gun, the MP 40, is commonly misidentified by the nomenclature - "Schmeisser." The MP 40 is distinguished from its predecessor, the MP 38, by the absence of the ribbed receiver. The 9mm ammunition for these weapons is the same as for the P 08 and P 38 pistol, both in service with airborne forces.

January 18 saw the arrival at Anzio of 50,000 U.S. and British troops under command of U.S. Major-General Lucas. While no appreciable opposition had been met during the initial stages of the landing, Lucas held his forces back to consolidate the beachhead. During this intervening period of several days, Kesselring reinforced those units already present and when the Allied advance tried to resume, they found the Germans were not to be budged.

Heavily committed to the battle for Cassino, new **Fallschirmjäger** personnel would also shortly be involved in the battle for Italy at Anzio. The **4. Fallschirmjäger-Division,** formed in northern Italy from a cadre of **2. Fallschirmjäger-Division** and former members of the Italian **"Folgore"** and **"Dembo"** Parachute Divisions (Italy had by this time surrendered to the Allies) in November 1943, had been transfered to add their numbers to the defending forces in Anzio. The **3.**

Allied air superiority had broken the back of German forces at the Salerno beachhead and would thereafter pose a serious threat to any German movement, troop or supplies. Local solutions to the supply problem and their movement were often found as exampled here.

A heavy MG 42 in action.

Fallschirmjäger-Division, created in October 1943 near Reims, France, remained in western Europe for the remainder of the war. Destroyed in the Normandie-Falaise area, 3rd Parachute Division, recreated again in Belgium, fell to the Allies in the Ruhr area in April 1945. Units of the **"Hermann Göring"** Division were likewise found in the Anzio area.

A major counterattack, planned by Kesselring, to drive the Allies off the beaches at Anzio almost proved fatal for the Allies. On February 18 only a little more than five miles separated the advance German forces from Anzio. The five weak German divisions containing the beachhead area lacked the resources and their offensive energies had been spent, Kesselring had been compelled to call off the assault. During the months of March and April, the beachhead lay quiet, both sides rested to regain strength. Reintensified efforts on the part of the Allies to crack Monte Cassino and Anzio began in the middle of May, this time the defense lines crumbled. Rome fell on June 4.

Ever pressing, British and U.S. forces along with Polish and French units, forced a steady retreat by German forces further and further north. The 1st and 4th Parachute Divisions would play important parts during the withdrawal and in the defensive battles of Florence, Rimini, Bologna and along the Po river. On May 2, 1945 surrender of Army Group C ended their struggle.

■ ■ ■

Employing a **8cm Kurzer Granatenwerfer 42** (81mm short mortar) this mortar crew directs its fire on advancing Allied units. It can not be said for a fact that these particular men belong to the **SS-Fallschirmjäger** force even though two crew members wear Waffen-SS camouflage field jackets, often times men wore what could be found. A classic example of this is a German sailor in the Mediterranean wearing an Army splinter camouflage jacket, Luftwaffe tropical pants and Navy blue service cap!

Two **SS-Fallschirmjäger** battalions are known to have existed, **SS-Fallschirmbataillone Nr. 500 and 501**. Additional personnel, jump qualified, could have been attached to special commands thoroughout SS formations. One combat jump has been credited to the SS-Paratroopers, a raid on Tito's headquarters at Drvar in May 1944. The mission failed when Tito managed to escape. The uniform for SS-paratroopers was the same as for the Luftwaffe with the exception that the jump smock appeared in SS camouflage patterns and colors.

A Sturmgeschütz III of the I./Fallschirm-Sturmgeschutz-Brigade 12 in Wilkowischken, Russia, 1944. The most successful Panzerjager of the Fallschirmtruppe (troops) was Leutnant Heinz Deutsch of the I. Batterie F. Stu G. Brig. 12 who received the Knight-Cross for destroying 44 enemy tanks.

Gran Sasso
September 12, 1943

Additional development of the DFS 230 glider lead to a parachute pack being installed in the tail section of the aircraft allowing it to dive at a steeper angle. Later, forward firing braking rockets were fitted to the nose. Both devices provided a much shortened landing space. The 230 gliders used on the Gran Sasso raid were fitted with both pieces of equipment.

The hotel Camp d'Imperatore on the Gran Sasso in which Mussolini was held prisoner.

One of the DFS 230 gliders which carried the men of Operation **Eiche,** code name for the Mussolini rescue, to the hotel Camp d'Imperatore's front door. Little flat area surrounded the hotel and made the landing of the gliders difficult, fullest use of the para-brake and braking rockets had to be made.

Fallschirmjägergewehr 42 (FG 42).

The daring raid to rescue Il Duce had come as a direct order from Hitler. The military aspects of the mission were entrusted to General Student. **Fallschirmjäger-Lehrbataillon** under command of Major Mors had been assigned the difficult task of conducting the mission itself. **SS-Hauptsturm-fuhrer** Otto Skorzeny, to the right of Il Duce, had been responsible for locating Mussolini but later assumed all credit for the rescue.

Posing for photos before his departure, by various stops, to Hitler's Headquarters, Mussolini appears somewhat grim while surrounded by jubilant rescuers. Skorzeny, dressed in a tropical Luftwaffe Captain's uniform, stands to his right and to the right of Skorzeny is Major Mors. Twenty-six members of Skorzeny's Waffen-SS detachment accompanied the Luftwaffe men, all wore Air Force uniforms and equipment.

The Fallschirmjäger Gewehr 42 (FG 42) assault rifle had been intended to replace the rifle, submachine gun and light machine gun in airborne formations. Its first appearance in combat took place on the Gran Sasso raid, Operation **Eiche.** Initial tests in the field indicated some undesirable traits and few of the first model were produced. A second improved model appeared in 1944 and became a highly regarded weapon. Owing to conditions at the end of the war only a small number of the FG 42 were produced. A special eight pocket bandolier, shown, accommodated the 20 round 7.92mm magazine clip.

Prior to his departure, Il Duce talks with General Soleti, a senior officer of the **carabinieri.** Soleti had been forced at gun point to accompany the Germans on the mission so that he could talk with Mussolini's **carabinieri** Guards and prevent undue actions on their part.

Mission complete. Mussolini, Skorzeny and the pilot of the "Storch," Captain Gerlach (General Student's personal pilot) prepare to leave the Gran Sasso. The unserviceability of the cable car leading to the hotel prompted use of the reliable Fieseler Fi 156, making full use of its reputation of short landings and take-offs.

Members of the **Nachrichtenzug,** communications section, are attached to each headquarters unit. Keeping the lines of communication open during the opening of the French invasion at Normandie proved difficult as French underground units attempted to isolate various German defending groups.

Part of a **Maschinegewehr-Kompanie,** machine gun company, on the Cotentin peninsula, 6th Regiment, 2 Parachute Division. Due to the high rate of fire of the MG 42, barrels had to be changed often, a spare barrel container lays in front of the machine gun. The fighting ability of the "new" airborne forces continued to show itself well above normal and they gave an excellent accounting of themselves. Their inability to stop the Allies on the beachhead is not a fault of their own actions but rather the OKW who refused to release additional Panzer units, fearing Normandie was only a feint by the Allies.

Men of the U.S. 29th Infantry Division captured in the fighting outside St. Lo are questioned by an English speaking member of the 5th Parachute Division. An important part of the fighting in and about St. Lo was shared by the 3rd and 5th Parachute Divisions.

Wearing the **Feldgendarmerie** (Field Police) gorget, this **Oberfeldwebel** (Master Sergeant) leads captured U.S. 29th Division infantrymen behind the lines. Note should be made that while the **Oberfeldwebel** is a member of an airborne unit he lacks the Parachutists' Badge, indicating the slowly deteriorating state of training within the parachute arm.

Final respects are paid by two companions of **Unteroffizier** Wilhelm Küster killed in action on June 16, 1944. Many more **Fallschirmjägers** would fall before the closing battles of the Second World War. 2nd, 3rd and 5th Parachute Divisions would bleed to death in Normandie and after reformation in Belgium and Holland, die a second death in the Ruhr and Ardennes.

Fallschirmjäger Monument on Crete

CENTER FOLD COLOR PLATE

Plate I Hauptmann and Jäger, Holland, 1940
During the early stages of German airborne operations and development of operational equipment and uniforms, few variations existed in the **Fallschirmjager** dress. The older style Army paratroop jump suit with two zippers running diagonally up the front and with no pockets, remained in use alongside the "1st pattern" **Luftwaffe** smock. Differences in the **Luftwaffe** model centered about the number of pockets contained in the garment. The kneeling **Hauptmann** (Captain), left, has three zip pockets, two chest high and one on the thigh, while the wounded **Jäger**, right, has but two. Also of note is the fact that the Army style breast eagle remains on the private's smock indicating that he has recently transferred from the Army to the **Luftwaffe**. A covered pocket in the right trouser leg, visible below the lower edge of the **Jäger's** smock, carried the paratrooper's "gravity knife", a standard flight crew piece of equipment. The knife would be used to clear fouled harness or shroud lines and on occasion for self-defense. The web fabric bandolier worn about the neck contains 105 rounds of 7.92mm rifle ammo for the **Kar 98K**. The **Hauptmann's** signal pistol (**Leuchtpistole**) is carried in a special pocket on the back right side of his jump suit. Both men are armed with the **Luger P 08** pistol. Side lace brown jump boots are worn at this time. A newer model front lace jump boot was introduced after the close of the Crete Campaign.

Plate II Obergefreiter, Crete, May 1941
A young **Obergefreiter** (Corporal) prepares for the drop on Crete by pulling his jump smock over his flight blouse. Until the end of 1940, the flight blouse, usually worn beneath the jump smock, possessed no side pockets. Requests from troops in the field brought about the addition of the two pockets. The blouse was secured by a single row of hidden buttons. The **Luftwaffe** version of the national emblem, a spread winged eagle holding the swastika and flying towards the right, is worn over the right breast while the **Fallschirmjager** badge is worn on the left side. Note should be made that the **Luftwaffe** emblem decal used on the steel helmets featured a reversed pose of the spread winged eagle, that is flying towards the left. Use of the national colors decal on steel helmets of all branches of the **Wehrmacht** began to be phased out about this time. The Corporal's insignia of rank is denoted by the three metal wings on the collar patches and also by the double chevron worn on the left arm. The gold-yellow "Waffenfarbe" of the flying troops, common to both flight personnel and paratroops, is most evident on the collar patches and the edged shoulder straps of his blouse. Black laceless jump boots complete his uniform.

Plate III Fallschirmjager, Crete, May 1941
Both the **Luftwaffe** "1st pattern" and "2nd pattern" jump smocks were in use during the invasion of Crete. Here a machine gunner rests during a lull in the battle. He wears the "1st pattern" smock which has permanently tailored legs, step-in, and two large zippered pockets located at the thighs. The tan colored helmet cover provides bands over the top of the helmet and around the side to facilitate the addition of foliage for camouflage purposes. Secured to his waist belt of brown leather, the entrenching tool is held in place by a loop stitched to the left thigh of the smock. Also worn on the belt is the holster for his **Walther P 38** pistol, the holster incorporates a holder for spare magazines, and his canteen and cup, not visible. A sweat rag of parachute material circles his neck and a 50 round belt of 7.92mm ammunition for the **MG 34** drapes over his shoulder. Blue-grey **Fallschirmjager** trousers are secured into the tops of the side lace brown jump boots. The tropical uniform was not introduced into service until after the Crete Campaign. The first camouflage pattern jump smock had been introduced into service by the spring of 1940 and two variants of this saw use on Crete, the "splinter" and "splotch" patterns, both became standard issue thereafter. An additional supply of ammunition is contained in the cannister at the gunner's feet.

Plate IV Fallschirmjager Trainee, Stendal Airbase, 1942
The parachute training of **Fallschirmjager** occupied approximately eight weeks. Within the first few days the fledgling became completely familiar with the parachute, each being required to pack his own 'chute. Here a new recruit prepares for his first jump. The jump smock "2nd pattern" is tightly buttoned about the thighs so as to not foul the 'chute harness which is just being fastened. The static line atop the 'chute pack will automatically open the parachute after exiting the aircraft. Great care is taken to insure that this line will not become tangled, as German paratroopers carried no reserve 'chute. Rubber knee pads are in place and additional pads will be added to the elbows. These protective devices could be a life saving piece of equipment. The life expectancy of a paratrooper injured during a combat jump could be extremely short. The **Fallschirmjager** steel helmet was also rubber lined and featured the forked chin-harness.

Plate V Generalmajor and Feldwebel, North Africa, 1942
The tropical uniform, as worn by **Generalmajor** (Major General) Ramcke, left, is typical of that worn by all ranks with the exception of his gold colored insignia of rank and **Luftwaffe** eagle. A white eagle would be found for other officer and enlisted ranks. The uniform was generally issued with tunic, bloused or long pants, lace up boots or shoes and field cap. The General is wearing the white officer's summer service cap in place of the field cap. For five months of the year the tropical uniform could be worn within the continental borders of Germany and was year round service dress in the Mediterranean area. Next to his parachutist badge, the General displays the Iron Cross First Class, with the **Ritterkruz**, Knight's Cross of the Iron Cross, suspended from his neck. In his button hole is the 1939 Bar to the 1914 Iron Cross. The **Feldwebel** (Technical Sergeant) has changed his paratroop helmet for a regular **Wehrmacht** type with net camouflage cover. The camouflaged shelter quarter was a dual purpose piece of equipment. Being waterproof, it served in its initial function as being one quarter of a pyramid shaped tent, thus the name, or it could be worn as a poncho style rain coat by slipping one's head through a slit in the center as is demonstrated by the sergeant. Both the right and left spare **MP 40** ammo pouches are being worn by the **Feldwebel**, enabling him to carry six 32 round 9mm box magazines for his weapon. Two **Stielhandgranate 24** (high explosive stick grenade) have been placed with their handles in his web belt for quick accessibility.

Plate VI Oberfeldwebel and Oberleutnant, Italy 1943-44
Outfitted in assault gear—mess can, rolled shelter quarter in "splotch" pattern, gas mask cannister, canteen and cup, entrenching tool and **Brotbeutel** ("bread bag") for personal necessities—this **Oberfeldwebel** (Master Sergeant), left, wears the late model jump smock closed about the legs, the snap fittings of which are clearly seen. Insignia of rank has been left off the smock. Armed with an **FG 42**, late model, a weapon intended to replace the rifle, sub-machine gun and light machine gun in paratroop units but produced in small numbers. The sergeant's ammunition is carried in a special bandolier, holding eight 20 round clips of standard 7.92mm rifle ammunition, worn about the neck. His helmet has been finished in olive green, an alternate to **Luftwaffe** blue; tan colored helmets were another option. Steel chicken wire has been used to assist in placing camouflage foliage onto the helmet, a common practice. The **Oberleutnant**, right, also wears the late smock in the closed position. Generally, when on the ground the closing snaps of this "2nd pattern" smock were left open for increased movement. Both the "splinter" and "splotch" pattern camouflage were issued in different predominant camouflage colors, brown or green, to better conceal during the various seasons. The **M1943** cap, a visored soft cap based on the mountain troop's cap, was introduced into Air Force service in 1943 and is worn by the Lieutenant. An Army issue black map case is attached to his belt, note the double claw officer's buckle.

BACK COVER COLOR PLATE

Plate VII SS-Hauptsturmführer Otto Skorzeny and Fallschirmjäger, Gran Sasso Raid, 1943
During the **Gran Sasso** Raid, the rescue of Benito Mussolini, the then **SS-Hauptsturmfuhrer** (SS-Captain) Otto Skorzeny, left, wore a **Luftwaffe** tropical uniform complete with **Luftwaffe** insignia! Other **Waffen SS** men who participated in the raid wore **Luftwaffe** uniforms and insignia as well, including jump smocks, but usually with the regular **Wehrmacht** steel helmet. After the successful completion of the rescue mission, Skorzeny received a promotion to the rank of **Major**. The **Jager**, right, a member of the **Lehrbataillons** and whose members were the most numerous on this particular mission, carries an early model of the **Fallschirmjäger Gewehr 42, FG 42,** reportedly used in action for the first time during this operation. A limited number of the early model **FG 42** were produced and it is distinguished by its stamped metal stock. It was not until 1944 that all the teething troubles were overcome and production again commenced on the weapon. The later model featured a wooden or plastic stock. The eight pocket ammunition bandolier is clearly seen. Both the rifle and **FG 42** ammunition bandoliers were issued in green, blue-grey or camouflaged patterns. A large opening net has been used on the **Jager's** helmet for camouflage application and is secured to his helmet by means of an elastic strap.

Plate VIII Oberleutnant, Mussolini Rescue Mission, 1943
This member of the **Fallschirmjäger Lehrbatallions** wears his "splinter" pattern jump smock over a tropical uniform. The tropical uniform pants were somewhat baggier that the former blue-grey **Fallschirmjäger** trousers and are fastened snugly around the boot with an ankle strap and buckle. The two wing and single bar insignia, viewed on the right arm, indicates this officer's rank as that of **Oberleutnant** (1st Lieutenant). The steel helmet, which had been worn during the glider assault landing on the **Gran Sasso**, has been replaced with a regular officer's service cap. General equipment for the raid was held to a minimum, emphasis being placed on armament and ammunition as serious resistance had been expected of Mussolini's guards. Only three spare **MP 40** ammunition pouches are worn, these being made of canvas material. These pouches were available in pairs, a distinct set of three for the right and left sides, and were issued in light green, light chocolate brown or wheat (illustrated) material as well as in leather. The canteen cover is tan felt, for tropical uniforms; standard **Luftwaffe** blue-grey canteen covers have been seen in use with tropical uniforms.

Plate IX Unteroffizier, Normandie, June 1944
This **Unteroffizier** (Sergeant) of the **6th Fallschirmjager Regiment, 2nd Division,** shows the strain of the hard fought battles in the Normandy beachhead area. **6th Regiment** distinguished itself while opposing U.S. paratroopers who landed the night of 6 June on the Cotentin peninsula. The "2nd pattern" jump smock is being worn open to provide greater ease of movement and features the "splotch" camouflage pattern. The rolled shelter quarter, seen directly above the canteen and cup, is in the "splinter" geometric pattern. The helmet cover, while of the same camouflage material as the smock, has no provisions for camouflage bands or loops. This problem has been remedied by "field methods," the use of a plain leather strap to hold foliage in place on the helmet. The normal insignia of rank worn on the smock, a single grayish wing, has been deleted, a practice common during the closing days of the war. The complete insignia of rank on the blouse is all but covered by the smock. If this insignia were visible, however, it would consist of a single aluminum metal wing on the gold-yellow collar patch with sergeant's "lace", aluminum fabric, surrounding both the collar and shoulder strap. Black Army issue rifle ammunition pouches and belt have been mixed with the regulation **Luftwaffe** enlistedman's belt buckle, rectangular shaped of matt aluminum with the **Luftwaffe** eagle surrounded by a laurel wreath. The mixing of Army and **Luftwaffe** equipment had been necessary due to general shortages.

Plate X Fallschirmjäger, Winter 1944-45
Of the two **Fallschirmjäger** divisions which took part in the German Ardennes offensive (Battle of the Bulge) approximately 1,200 men, who comprised "**Kampfgruppe von der Heydte**", took part in the actual air drop phase. The remainder of the parachute forces committed to the battle operated in a normal ground assault role. The uniform of this **Jager** (Private), a member of the **5. Fallschirmjäger Divisionen,** is typical of those of the period, paratroops in a strict infantry function. Over the top of his standard **Luftwaffe** blue-grey overcoat he wears a ¾ length camouflaged smock in a muted pattern of autumn browns, "splotch" pattern. An identical smock was worn by **Luftwaffe-Felddivisionen,** Air Force Field Divisions, who fought exclusively as infantry. Normal equipment harness is worn, **Luftwaffe** brown, although at this late date an influx of Army black leather gear has been noted. Another "infantry" influence viewed, is the use of leggings with the black high shoes, a method adopted to circumvent the shortages of leather. Spare magazines for the **Jäger's MP 43** are carried in the large pockets of the smock. Leather gloves, often replaced with wool mittens or even stockings, and wearing a toque under the paratroop helmet provided added protection against the harsh winter weather.